DISCOVERING AUSTRALIAN
WILDLIFE

A LITTLE AUSTRALIAN GIFT BOOK

www.steveparish.com.au

DISCOVERING AUSTRALIAN WILDLIFE

Australia's millions of years of isolation from other continents, and the variety of habitats it offers, have contributed to the uniqueness of its wild creatures.

Many of the continent's furry animals are marsupials, whose young are born bald, blind and helpless and complete their development safe in their mother's warm pouch. Marsupials come in all sizes and shapes, from the giant Red Kangaroo to the tiny pygmy-possums. Koalas and wombats are particular favourites of people from all over the world.

Even more fascinating than the marsupials are the two egg-laying species of mammals, the Platypus and the echidna. The Platypus is found only in waterways, while the echidna may be found anywhere it can find termites to eat.

Australia has approximately 700 species of birds, including some of the world's most magnificent parrots, the huge, flightless Emu and large numbers of waterbirds.

The roll-call of remarkable wildlife includes reptiles, frogs, insects and a diversity of marine and freshwater life.

This book is an introduction to a few of Australia's most fascinating wild creatures.

Title page:

Sugar Glider

Opposite:

Koalas eat the leaves of a limited number of eucalypt tree species. They sleep most of the day and are active mainly at night.

COMMON WOMBAT

It is a pity wombats do not spend more daylight time in the open, for they are delightful animals, intelligent and full of personality. However, while the sun shines they are usually curled up asleep underground in their burrows. They occasionally emerge to feed on dull, overcast days, but usually confine their public appearances to after dark.

The burrow is the centre of wombat life. A number of wombats may share a burrow system, but, apart from mothers living with dependent young ones, each wombat has its own living quarters and goes its separate way through the bush.

Opposite:

A Common Wombat grazing on an overcast day.

Left:

A Common Wombat wandering its home range.

KOALA

A Koala is well adapted to life high in the treetops. The two thumbs on each of its powerful paws enable the Koala to hold tight to even the most slippery branches, while its dense fur shields it from rain and sun. If the Koala wishes to dine, it only has to reach out to secure a tasty sprig of fresh eucalypt leaves.

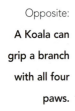

Opposite:
A Koala can grip a branch with all four paws.

Right:
A Koala reaches for a sprig of eucalypt leaves.

PARROTS

Australia is known as "the land of parrots", for it is home to many species of these brilliantly coloured birds and their larger, crested relatives, the cockatoos. In some parrots, such as the Australian King-Parrot, the males and females are coloured so differently that they are often mistaken for separate species.

Opposite:

This is a male Australian King-Parrot. The female has a green head and breast.

Left:

The Crimson Rosella has a chiming call.

WALLABIES AND KANGAROOS

Wallabies, kangaroos and their relatives move about slowly by leaning forward, and placing both front paws on the ground. Then they push themselves forward with hind legs and tail. When alarmed, they rise on their powerful hind legs and race away in long, hopping bounds. Scientific study shows that this remarkable gait actually takes less effort than the gallop of an animal that uses all four legs when moving at speed.

A wallaby is simply a small kangaroo.

Opposite:
An Eastern Grey Kangaroo.

Left:
This young Bennett's Wallaby is ready to leave the pouch for good.

POSSUMS

Many possums live in trees, and have grasping hands and feet and long, flexible tails which aid in climbing through the branches. A few species live in rocky habitats. As their large, forward-gazing eyes suggest, all possums are active at night.

Possums fill many niches in Australia's bushland habitats. The Common Ringtail Possum can be found in all states except the Northern Territory in dense vegetation. Pygmy-possums live in Australia's south-east, curling up in leafy nests in hollow branches during daytime and feeding on nectar and insects at night.

Opposite:
The Common Ringtail Possum has a curling, prehensile tail.

Right:
An Eastern Pygmy-possum feeding on nectar.

WATERBIRDS

Water is a precious resource over most of Australia and waterbirds may have to travel long distances from one swamp or billabong to another. Yet when heavy rain falls in the far inland, waterbirds will fly in within days, intent upon nesting and raising young. They must get their offspring to flying stage before the water evaporates under the relentless outback sun, or they will not survive.

Opposite:

Australian Pelican

Left:

Plumed Whistling-Duck

FROGS

When rain falls anywhere in Australia, male frogs emerge from their hiding places in holes, burrows and swamps and begin calling for mates. Their voices resound until their pleas are answered. Then a new generation of eggs hatches into tadpoles which will, in turn, metamorphose into smaller replicas of their parents.

Opposite:
Dainty Green Tree-frog calling for a partner.

Right:
Green Tree-frogs mating.

TASMANIAN DEVIL

The inquisitive air of the Tasmanian Devil portrayed on this page is probably more typical of this dog-sized marsupial than the gaping jaws opposite. Such a fierce expression is usually an attempt to intimidate a fellow Devil and filch a few mouthfuls of tasty roadkill or other easily obtained meal.

The Tasmanian Devil is very much a part of contemporary Tasmanian life and may even be seen scavenging on the outskirts of country towns.

Opposite and left: **A Tasmanian Devil displays its truly remarkable gape. However, it is no match for a determined dog in a fight.**

SHORT-BEAKED ECHIDNA

The echidna wanders around the bush, digging up ants and termites with its powerful clawed paws and flipping them into its tiny mouth with its long, sticky tongue.

Faced with danger, an echidna scrabbles frantically at the ground beneath it and, if the surface is sufficiently soft, rapidly sinks downwards, protected by its coat of bristling spines. When the coast is clear, it emerges again and trundles off in search of still more termites.

Opposite:

The damp snout of this questing Short-beaked Echidna contains tiny electro-receptors which detect the presence of termite prey.

Left:

An echidna sinking into the sand to escape.

LIZARDS

Two of Australia's most spectacular lizards belong to the group called dragons. These fast-moving reptiles have strong legs, long tails and skins covered with tiny scales. Many also have frills of skin on their necks or down their backs.

The Frilled Lizard carries the ruff to extremes, using it to scare away attackers, intimidate other 'Frillies' and to pass off excess heat from its body on warm tropical days.

The Southern Forest Dragon's crest and lichen-coloured scales allow it to blend with tree trunks. Clinging motionless to a rainforest tree, it is remarkably difficult to see.

Opposite:
The Frilled Lizard is found across northern Australia.

Right:
The Southern Forest Dragon is a rainforest species.

EMU

Widespread on mainland Australia, Emus are flightless birds that escape danger by running. Their shaggy plumage is made up of double-shafted, filamentous feathers. After the female lays a clutch of dark green eggs, the male incubates them and then looks after the chicks for the next 18 months.

Opposite:
Emus may be seen in open bushland and on plains.

Right:
The Emu features on the Australian Coat of Arms.

PLATYPUS

With its dense fur, and eyes and nostrils on top of its head, the Platypus is adapted for life in water. The feet are webbed, though, as shown here, the webbing can be turned under when the platypus travels on land or digs into a river bank to make a resting or nesting burrow.

A female Platypus lays two soft-shelled eggs, which she curls around until they hatch into naked babies. These feed on milk produced by glands on their mother's belly until they are furred and ready to hunt underwater on their own.

Opposite:
This Platypus will hunt underwater with its eyes closed, its bill sensing small water animals by the electrical discharges from their bodies.

Left:
A Platypus is superbly adapted for aquatic living.

DINGO

'Yellow-dog-dingo' (which may be black, ginger or white) is part of Australian legend, but there is no evidence of dingos on the continent before around 3500 years ago. Dingos probably came to Australia with seafarers from South-East Asia at around that time.

Opposite:
The Dingo is Australia's largest predator.

Left:
Dingo family territories usually include a source of water.

LAUGHING KOOKABURRA

This familiar bushland resident has adapted to town life and is often seen perching on fence, branch or wire. It lives in groups, which greet the dawn with a chorus of laughing, chuckling calls, staking their claim to the family territory. An adult pair of kookaburras will raise their chicks assisted by a number of younger birds, their offspring from past years.

Opposite:
The Laughing Kookaburra is a giant kingfisher.

Right:
This Laughing Kookaburra is alert for a lizard, frog or earthworm.

INDEX TO ANIMALS PICTURED

Devil, Tasmanian 18, 19
Dingo 28, 29
Dragon, Southern Forest 22
Echidna, Short-beaked 20, 21
Emu 24, 25
Kangaroo, Eastern Grey 10
King-Parrot, Australian 8
Koala 2, 6, 7
Kookaburra, Laughing 30, 31
Lizard, Frilled 23
Numbat 32

Pelican, Australian 14
Platypus 26, 27
Possum, Common Ringtail 13
Pygmy-possum, Eastern 12
Rosella, Crimson 9
Sugar Glider 1
Tree-frog, Dainty Green 17
Tree-frog, Green 16
Wallaby, Bennett's 11
Whistling-Duck, Plumed 15
Wombat, Common 4, 5

Right:
Numbat